MW01035421

GARABANDAL

AND

ITS SECRETS

The Warning and the Miracle of Garabandal,
Like Nothing Before in History —
Two Supernatural Events That Will Change the World —
the Global Reset — Heaven Resets on Their Terms

By Ted Flynn

Maxkol Communications

For those who wish to get more information on Garabandal, order from Signs and Wonders for Our Times: *The Thunder of Justice, the Warning, the Miracle, the Chastisement, the Era of Peace,* the international best seller by Ted & Maureen Flynn.

Published and printed in the USA
© MaxKol, 2022
ISBN Number: 978- 0-9634307-8-6
Design Layout: Paul McNamara

Publisher:
MAXKOL, All rights reserved

For bulk or case orders **contact: tflynn333@icloud.com**

Distributor:
Signs and Wonders of Our Time
P.O Box 345
Herndon, Virginia 20170
E mail: signsorders@gmail.com
Phone: (703) 707-0799
Website: Sign.org

DEDICATED TO

Our Lady of Mount Carmel

This book of the law shall not depart out of your mouth,
but you shall meditate on it day and night,
that you may be careful to do according to all that is
written in it; for then you shall make yourself prosperous,
and then you shall have good success.

JOSHUA 1:8

Men of Israel, hear these words Jesus of Nazareth,
a man attested to you by God with mighty works
and wonders and signs which God did through Him
in your midst, as you yourselves know.

ACTS 2:22

Have no anxiety about anything, but in everything
by prayer and supplication with thanksgiving
let your request be made to God. And the peace of God,
which passes all understanding, will keep your hearts
and your minds in Christ Jesus. Finally, brethren,
whatever is true, whatever is honorable, whatever is just,
whatever is pure, whatever is lovely, whatever is gracious,
if there is any excellence, if there is anything
worthy of praise, think about these things.

PHIL. 4: 6-8

Table of Contents

The Warning and the Great Miracle of Garabandal, Like Nothing Before in History — Two Supernatural Events That Will Change the World — The Global Reset — Heaven Resets on Their Terms

And I will work wonders in the heavens above, and signs on the earth below; blood, fire, and a cloud of smoke. (Acts 2:19).

Listen to me, you devout sons of mine, and blossom like a rosebush on a stream bank. Bloom like a sweet-smelling lily, and send your fragrance into the air like incense. Sing the Lord's praise and thank Him for all that He has done.... All that the Lord has done is very good: all that He commands is sooner or later done. No one should ask why things are as they are; these questions will be answered at the right time: whatever He commands is promptly done; there are no limits to His power to save.... He sees the whole of time, from the beginning to end, and nothing takes Him by surprise. No one should ask why things are as they are; everything in creation has its purpose. (Sirach 39:13-21).

For those familiar with Signs and Wonders Magazine, and my writings, I have had a particular interest in the apparitions of the Blessed Mother at Garabandal Spain since the mid 1980's. Garabandal has a uniqueness all its own, about which I have written extensively. My wife Maureen and I released a book in 1993 (revised in 2010), ***The Thunder of Justice, The Warning, the Miracle, the Chastisement, The Era of Peace.*** The story and messages of Garabandal were the heart and the soul of the book. Garabandal is a fascinating story historically, prophetically, scripturally, and mystically. It lays the tiles together for a beautiful mosaic of Heaven's language to their people. Garabandal points to future events that are complimentary to other elements in the Catholic faith, as well as significant events that are in the Old Testament. If one understands that God, the Blessed Mother, and the Host of Heaven, have a plan for the salvation of all mankind in our troubled times, then Garabandal and its promises make even more sense.

My wife and I first visited Garabandal in 1994, and again in 2017 on pilgrimage to Fatima (its 100th anniversary). Garabandal was an eye-opening experience on the second visit, because we had learned so much more during that interval of time since our first visit. What was most noticeable in 2017 was how little had changed in the village. More accurately, we were stunned by it. The church had not been updated or expanded, and was still tiny, and only a few dozen more homes were built. For pilgrims, there were only two public bathrooms. Two! It was eerie in its simplicity and remoteness from the noise of the world, and what is expected to happen there at some point in the future. The miraculous that is prophesied to happen there will be unprecedented in all of history. The lack of amenities and facilities may be a part of the much bigger story when the Miracle does happen.

The Push for a Great Reset

At a point in time there are continual changes the way societies and civilizations govern and rule — and who the new governing powers will be. To have a new one, there will be one replaced. This is the story of civilization itself that historians like Will Durant and others wrote about. We see empires like Egypt under the Pharaohs, Persia, the Greeks, Alexander the Great, the Romans, Spain under the Armada, France under the Sun Kings, England sailing the seven seas for commodities and spices, and America after World War II and Bretton Woods, becoming the undisputed ruler of finance and industry globally in the twentieth century. However, never has the world seen an integrated and interconnected community of nations like we now see. It is a new phase of mankind. With so many government bodies vying for control, we see any nation that steps out of bounds from what a global elite deems appropriate, then that nation will be doomed to either obscurity or destruction. At the heart of it all is who controls central banking. On March 21, 2022 President Joseph Biden gave another indication we are in a seismic shift as nations in the past when he said, *"you know we are in an inflection point, I believe in the world economy. Not just the economy, the world. It occurs every three or four generations. As one of the top military generals told me the other day in a secure meeting, 60 million people died between 1900 and 1946, and since then we have established a liberal world order and that hadn't happened in a long while. Lot of people dying now, but nowhere near the chaos. And now's the time when things are shifting.* **There's gonna be a new world order out there, and we've gotta lead it. And we've gotta unite the rest of the world in doing it."**

A Reset Designed by God

All over the news is the Great Reset of the elites pushing their agenda of global control. However, the Warning and the Great Miracle of Garabandal will be Heaven's Reset on their own terms to offset the evil in our day. *Where sin abounds, grace abounds all the more* (Romans 5:20) Due to the interconnectivity of this community of nations, Heaven will have their own global solutions.

The breadth and width of the events of the prophetic events that are to occur at Garabandal are breathtaking and will defy natural law. At the time of this writing, there are five Cardinals and many bishops that are openly saying they see signs of the *"end times"* in our midst. More people of all faiths see we are in *"the end of times."* If one were to look at the world, mankind has run out of answers to govern itself. It is not a question of looking at the glass half full, it is seeing that mankind is on the precipice of destruction on a global basis. A spark from just about anywhere could ignite a world-wide maelstrom that could generate a massive tsunami of destruction. There would be uncontrollable wars were it not for the grace of Heaven to stop the carnage. The Blessed Mother told Sister Lucy of Fatima, *"Wars are a punishment for the sins of mankind."* The anxiety and commotion of our times are birthing a New Era. Any mother can tell you, it is a painful process before the birth of a child. The old is passing away, and New Times await us. Satan knows his time is short, thus the flurry of evil in our day. Garabandal will be a **Global Reset** not the **Great Reset** designed by men, and it will be on Heaven's terms like the world has never seen. It will offset the evil of our day, and it will happen in an instant and change the world as we know it. People will soon speak of **before** the Warning and Miracle and **after** the Warning and the Miracle. It will be like they designate centuries and millennia Before Christ (BC) and After Christ (AD).

THE GAMECHANGER —
Heaven Intervenes — The Warning, the Illumination of Conscience, the Life Review, a Judgment in Miniature, the Correction of Conscience

People who have followed what the Blessed Mother has said in the past at Garabandal Spain, have been waiting in joyful hope for several events. There are millions who have been exposed to literature what has been said long ago to recent mystics. Heaven has a tendency of never being late, but it never seems to be early. A prophecy will happen exactly as Heaven said it will happen if it is authentic, but not necessarily as we perceive it in our mind. The Lord's ways are not our ways. We have seen this at Guadalupe, Rue du Bac, Lourdes, Fatima, Akita, LaSalette, and other apparition sites. Heaven moves with a still small voice (I Kings 19:12), as Heaven is never in a hurry. God is a God of order, and He speaks to us gently and in small doses over a long period of time so we can absorb and internalize the message.

God's DNA is mercy and He will not abandon us. As Jesus was walking on the water in the Sea of Galilee in the midst of a storm, His words to his spiritually young apostles were, *"Fear not, it is I"* (Matt. 14:27). Very early in his pontificate

Saint John Paul II would often say especially to the young, *"there is nothing to fear,"* and *"fear not."* It was a constant theme during his pontificate.

Anxiety comes from a lack of spiritual simplicity and the lack of a prayer life. To grasp the magnitude of events coming our way will require letting go of the superfluous things from our lives. What is amusing is the talk of people being "preppers." What was once a cottage industry has gone mainstream with big business engaged. When the largest retailers in the country like Sam's Club, Walmart, Target, and Costco are carrying all types of dried food sold in volume that they cannot keep in stock, it is time to take notice that many don't have great comfort in the present system or in government. Guns and ammunition have never been sold like they have in the last few years as people feel there will be a breakdown of society and have decided to take more control for protection. People are now paying more attention knowing that the present way we are living is a prelude to disaster. Items are widely being sold for consumer use that are helpful if the electric grid goes down. Stress and anxiety are all around us.

People are heading to the woods in cabins looking for solace and safety as they build doomsday refuges, and there is even a TV show about it. The thinking is that the system may break down, and it doesn't take a genius to see it. If people have the resources and means to head to the woods, that is their prerogative. However, their motives must be clear on why they are doing it. If it is not to help others, it will fail and will be a useless enterprise. There is no hiding from what is coming our way. A person may postpone disaster, but not totally avoid it. There will be no ultimate safety for what lies ahead — only spiritual. A person may mitigate disaster in the short term, but living off the grid is not a long-term solution. The digital control government has today is just too vast for anyone to run and hide for a long period of time.

What is amazing with all the physical prepping, is that there is little talk of spiritual preparation, the greatest preparation of all which will keep us safe. The Blessed Mother has been clear, the refuge is in her Immaculate Heart. Few ever speak of the necessary preparation to protect one's family that are spiritual. The clergy as a whole are afraid of the subject of apparitions for several reasons. **One,** they will be marginalized if they speak of these, thus they fear that. They fear man more than God, and some are men pleasers rather than God pleasers. **Two,** their Bishops frown upon them speaking on unapproved apparitions like Medjugorje, Garabandal, and others. **Three,** they don't know much about Our Lady's appearances.

What is the Lord doing? Is there a timetable? What are we to expect? No one knows the precise answers to these questions, but we are not far off from momentous changes nearly impossible to wrap our head around if what has been spoken about is true. Heaven has provided us some important data for us to know that these events may not be far off. What we are being told is just before the events, there will be chaos and war in the world. Due to the rapid disintegration of the way the world has existed in the past, new structures of totalitarian government are being ushered in due to the breakdown we see around us. What you once knew is no longer, and the safety net of government is gone, or at least disintegrating rapidly and not working as originally implemented.

This is not the end of the world, but what you knew in the past will be over. We will move forward in a new direction. What worked in the past is not working now, and plans are afoot for global government that will add new dimensions at a dizzying pace. Most people will wilt under the changes, and not be able to adapt and cope unless they have spiritual formation prior to the events. The speed of it all will cause many to lose employment, marriages will break up for a variety of reasons, with the most notable, spouses not in unison on ideology of what is really happening. There will be loss of property, general confusion, and capitalism itself will be transformed due to the added power of civil bodies all over the world. Just look at the force of totalitarian government control over the vaccine issue. Free-market economies are being altered due to interference from regulatory bodies that will dictate how business is done. The globalist goal is to put people in a *digital cage* to monitor all activities. Systems are now in place to execute that plan. The goal is Agenda 2030 under the United Nations, with the ideology of the World Economic Forum and other large multi and transnational bodies behind it. Every area of life will be affected, and no one will come away unscathed from the changes.

Just when it appears all is lost, Heaven will not abandon its children. Heaven has a plan. There will be two events, which will happen one after the other. The first is called **THE WARNING.** There are many other terms for it among credible mystics, but other terms most commonly used are the **"Illumination of Conscience/Life Review/Judgment in Miniature/Correction of Conscience."** By and large some people may know of these events coming our way through friends and family, but it tends to be almost exclusively Catholics that have been receptive to it. Why? It has been the Blessed Mother as the Prophetess of our age saying it, preparing us for many years about what is to come. She has been appointed by the Most Holy Trinity for her task at this point in time, as we move to the culmination of the battle. Satan's cohort battling God's cohort for the soul of mankind. In Revelation 12 the Woman Clothed with the Sun is in battle as the Queen of Heaven and earth. By and large there is great prejudice against her from those who wish to dismiss her if she speaks. Good Catholics, including some priests, reject the messages when she speaks, or will only address her messages in hushed terms for fear of being marginalized by their congregations or confreres. As long as she remains silent, many are fine with that. The faithful will often venerate her as a symbol in history, but they will shun her when someone speaks of her majesty and work in the world. Many think her activity stopped at Fatima and refuse to address the last 100 years. Soon, there will be no getting around what she has been saying, as we will know the appointed time by the events themselves. The events will dictate we look into what has been said at so many of her apparition sites.

The **Warning / The Illumination of Conscience / Life Review / Judgment in Miniature / Correction of Conscience** is an event that was described in more detail at the apparition in Garabandal, Spain than any other place. The reason is that the statements were so precise on what will happen at some future date. Similar statements have been mentioned by other mystics, and it will be an event like no other. What is prophesied to happen is that every person in the world will see their soul as God sees it at judgment, *"a judgment in miniature."* Anyone who knows people who have experienced a life after death experience or near-death experience (NDE), know that they come back dramatically changed people. Many who have experienced such phenomena come back and tell of having seen Heaven, Hell, or Purgatory. These are impossible to explain aside from a personal encounter. Most are not open to these events being real, some are. It is a choice. But no one will escape this event of a *"judgment in miniature."* Today, it is a relatively small population who know of it, but soon it will be the entire world. Never in recorded history has there been such an event. There will be no denying what has taken place. Throughout history, the Lord works with small numbers like He did with Gideon to show the victory was His alone. We will be stripped naked before God and we will see our life like a slow-motion movie picture. We will have no response before a Divine loving God, other than acknowledgment of truth. Sins that are more grievous will go slower, such as where we have hurt people with words or actions, and see our sins of omission and commission. In the presence of that Divine Truth, we will have no response other than acceptance. We will be in so much light and love, we will have no rebuttal to the truth we have seen. Today God is our Savior, at death He will be our judge.

The Visionaries, The Story of Garabandal & Saint Michael the Archangel

Located in the Cantabrian Mountains of Northern Spain near the Bay of Biscay in a remote village called Garabandal, the Blessed Mother appeared to four young girls over 2,000 times from 1961-1965. It was during the time of Vatican II where significant changes were happening in the church. Some events were spoken of in detail by the Blessed Mother that have never been said so clearly and directly in the past. Why? Heaven must think that we are in need of such events to shock us back to God. At the end of the events, people will be on one side or the other, but not sitting on a fence. They will be hot or cold, for or against the things of God, but not neutral. It will be a time like no other in history.

San Sebastian de Garabandal was a tiny village of about 300 people in the Diocese of Santander, when the Blessed

Mother first appeared in 1961. At the time of the apparition there wasn't a motor with moving parts in the entire village. The townspeople were simple and very devout. About a quarter mile to the north on a high ridge, nine pine trees tower over the village, marking the spot where Our Lady frequently appeared, and the spot where a Great Miracle is prophesied to happen in the future at the nine pines. The nine pines are tucked in a valley that is a natural amphitheater where millions can comfortably sit and look down on them.

The story of Garabandal began on the evening of June 18, 1961, when the Archangel Michael appeared to four young girls. The visionaries were: Conchita Gonzalez (age twelve), Jacinta Gonzalez (age twelve), Mari Cruz Gonzalez (age eleven), none of whom are closely related, and Mari-Loli Mazon (age twelve). He made eight silent appearances during the following twelve days. On July 1, St. Michael finally spoke to announce that on the following day the Blessed Virgin Mary would appear to them as Our Lady of Mount Carmel. The Blessed Mother then appeared on July 2 to the children. July 2 was the Feast of the Ark of the Covenant in the old liturgical calendar. Our Lady is the New Ark of the Covenant. The Ark of the Covenant contained the signs of God's presence among His chosen people and was a physical sign of Yahweh's covenant with His people. Was Our Lady showing us that she had come to do battle when she came to Garabandal?

The apparitions were preceded by three interior calls, which the girls described as joys, each one becoming stronger. After the third call, the girls would come running from different parts of the village and would arrive at the same time in the place designated by Our Lady. They would then fall to their knees in ecstasy.

The four seers described Our Lady as a beautiful young woman about eighteen years of age. She wore a white dress with a blue mantle and a brown scapular on her right arm. On her head she wore a crown of twelve stars as she appears in Revelation 12. Her hair was deep brown and parted in the center. Her face was oval with a fine nose. The girls said, *"No other woman looks like her or sounds like her."*

Each apparition affirmed and amplified others, with similar themes on the importance of the Rosary, the Eucharist, the Mass, the Sacraments, and all that entails living a daily life in communion with God. Many who follow such events make a mistake thinking what has been said at one apparition site (although that may be the case) will necessarily carry over to another. What is the focus here is that there will be events coming from Garabandal that will show the world God's faithfulness to His people. The old must pass, before the new can come. Before every Easter Sunday comes Good Friday and the Church at this point in time is walking the road of Calvary. At the time of Noah, his was the only righteous family to escape the flood. Genesis gives us a graphic account of the sin. We saw the same in Sodom and Gomorrah, when it was only Lot, his wife, and two daughters who escaped the wrath of God. What most people do not realize is that Lot's daughters were both betrothed, and neither made the journey out of the city after being warned. They were told not to look back, but Lot's wife disobeyed the Lord's command by turning around, and she turned to a pillar of salt. The sin of disobedience has consequences.

Heaven has an agenda and it is filled with grace. We can either accept it, or fight it. It is a personal choice. If a person is unsure whether Garabandal is true, wisdom would say to remain quiet to not quench the work of the Holy Spirit. If it is not true, it won't matter. But if it is true, nothing you can do or say will stop it. This would be a similar situation to the words of the Rabbi Gamaliel when he told the Jews not knowing what to do after the death of Jesus, as they fought amongst themselves at Pentecost. Addressing the Sanhedrin he said, *"What I suggest, therefore, is that you leave these men alone and let them go. If this enterprise, this movement of theirs, is of human origin it will break up of its own accord; but if it does in fact come from God you will not only be unable to destroy them, but you might find yourselves fighting against God"* (Acts 5:38-39). What is going to take place at Garabandal is of such mind-numbing scope, it is actually impossible to fully comprehend it. The events will be **God's ultimate acts of mercy** on a scale the world has never seen before. The Warning and the Great Miracle are both separate and distinct events on different days, but linked as one. One will follow the other.

When one sees in the modern era what the Blessed Mother and the Host of Heaven are looking to accomplish at authentic and time-tested apparition sites, there is more of a complete understanding of what is happening in the world. The messages of Garabandal address these issues. They show what Heaven is doing to bring us to a new Era of Peace, a New Jerusalem, a New Epoch — New Times. This will not be the end of the world as one could make a derisive comment, but a line of demarcation where world events transition to a New Time. We have seen transitions in history like after the Bolshevik Revolution, the French Revolution, the American Revolution, the American Civil War, World War 1 and II, etc. This will be much larger with a far bigger and wider global impact.

This narrative will present a short synopsis of what happened and what is expected to happen when Our Lady came and foretold future events for the world and the church. Due to the poverty of space, many poignant and important aspects of the story cannot be told, nor many of the controversies. *There are approximately two thousand messages given over four years* and innumerable stories could be told, but the point of this narrative is principally on the Warning, and the Great Miracle — the why of it, and its impact on the world, although several key messages are provided.

Mystical Phenomena

During the apparitions, many mystical phenomena were witnessed. The girls were able to detect and recognize priests who came to the village dressed in civilian clothes, trying to conceal their identities. Many times, during the ecstatic walks, the visionaries would offer these priests their crucifix to be kissed. During one of Conchita's ecstasies in 1962, two priests were kneeling down in reverence. They were gently encouraged by Conchita to stand up, in order to emphasize the deep respect that Our Lady has for priests. She taught the children to greet the priest before greeting an angel, because a priest is more important, since only a priest can consecrate bread and wine into the Body and Blood of Christ during the Holy Sacrifice of the Mass.

On occasions the young girls were subjected by investigators to burns, spotlights in their eyes, and pin pricks without showing any physical response to pain. Reports indicate that four adult men had difficulty lifting one twelve-year-old girl, yet the girls could lift each other easily to kiss Our Lady goodbye. The apparitions were accompanied by other phenomena that seemed to defy natural law, such as ecstatic falls and running fast forward and backward over very rocky terrain. For detractors of this phenomena they may want to read the story of Balaam's donkey speaking for being treated harshly (Numbers 22:21-39). Thus, the phrase, *"out of the mouth of an ass."* It is not every day a donkey speaks. Stories in the Bible don't always follow logical or natural law, yet one can barely read Scripture and not see the supernatural.

Many religious objects were kissed by Our Lady. The visionaries, while in ecstasy, would return the objects to their rightful owners even though their owners were unknown to them. The seers claimed that Our Lady guided them to the right person. Our Lady promised: *"Through the kiss I have bestowed on these objects, my Son will perform miracles, wonders, and prodigies before and after the Great Miracle.*" The fulfillment of this promise has been realized by the many conversions and cures of terminally ill and addicted people around the world.

Another remarkable event emphasized at Garabandal was the importance of the Eucharist. An angel appeared bearing a golden chalice. In many photographs of Garbandal, a chalice is often suspended in mid-air. This was very common in the early years of the apparitions, as the Eucharist was central to the messages. The angel asked the children to think of the One whom they were going to receive. He taught them to recite the Confiteor (Latin for a penitential prayer said at the beginning of the Mass in prior years), after which he gave them Holy Communion. He also taught them to say the Anima Christi in thanksgiving.

These "Angelic Communions" were recorded on film, showing the movement of the girls lips, tongue, and throat. However, since these Hosts were only visible to the girls, many skeptics doubted that they were actually receiving Holy Communion. When questioned about where the Hosts came from, since only a priest could consecrate, the angel told them that the Hosts were taken from the tabernacle of the church. Therefore, a priest and not an angel had consecrated the Hosts.

On June 22, 1962, the angel told Conchita that God would perform a *"special miracle."* The people would be allowed to see the Sacred Host appear on Conchita's tongue at the moment she received Communion, in order that they might believe. Conchita's diary entry for June 30, 1962, stated: *"While I was in the pines I heard a voice which said that the Miracle would take place on the eighteenth of July."* The angel later instructed her to reveal this message fifteen days in advance. She was unable to receive Communion on the 18th, but did receive the mystical Communion at 1:40 AM on July 19th. This occurred in front of numerous witnesses and was filmed.

Priest Sees the Great Miracle, Father Luis Maria Andreu, S.J.

Highlighting the centrality of the priesthood to the messages of Garabandal, two priests' stories underscore that importance while emphasizing Our Lady's presence with supernatural phenomena.

Father Luis Maria Andreu, a thirty-eight-year-old Jesuit priest, was visiting Garabandal for the second time on August 8, 1961. Father Luis, while observing the visionaries during ecstasy, suddenly cried out, *"Milagro!"* four times. When driving home later that night with his friends, Father Luis said, *"What a wonderful present the Virgin has given me! How lucky we are to have a mother like that in Heaven! Today is the happiest day of my life!"* Shortly after, he lowered his head and died. In a later apparition, Our Lady told the visionaries that Father Luis had seen her and had also seen the Great Miracle. He died of joy with his last words, *"This has been the happiest day of my life."* Our Lady also revealed to Conchita on September 14, 1965, that Father

Luis' body will be exhumed and found to be incorrupt on the day after the Great Miracle. Note this will be even more of a miracle since his remains were transferred and found to be decomposed.

Father Ramon Andreu, S.J., the brother of the deceased Father Luis Andreu, S.J., was also a significant witness whose life was dramatically changed by the events of Garabandal. He was privileged to have witnessed more than 400 ecstasies. During his visits to the village, he kept a detailed record in his notebooks of everything he saw and heard. These notebooks represent some of the more valuable documentation. The most startling event for Father Ramon was the revelation from the visionaries that they had conversed with his dead brother, Father Luis. Father Ramon was told precise details of his brother's funeral and details of his personal life that were unknown to anyone but himself. On another occasion, Father Luis gave a message for his mother: *"Be happy and content for I am in Heaven and I see you every day."* This was a message of great joy for his mother, who entered the convent, and a remarkable revelation about our loved ones who have gone to Heaven. He and his brother, Father Luis, were especially chosen by Our Lady to bear witness to the incredible events of Garabandal.

Support for the Apparitions

The apparitions were contemporaneous with Vatican II. Although there exist some differences of opinion among bishops. Since 1961, the Church has never condemned them. However, bishops have held different levels of interest and openness to the apparitions. The early position by one bishop was one of caution and the apparitions were dismissed with the whole affair as *"child's play."* In 1961, Our Lady told the visionaries: *"A time will come when all four of you will contradict yourselves one with the other, when your families will also contradict themselves about the apparitions; you will even deny that you have seen me or Saint Michael."* On this occasion witnesses heard the four visionaries while in ecstasy say: *"How is it that one day we will say that we did not see you, since we are seeing you now?"* Our Lady told them: *"Because you are going to pass through the same confusion as the Church."*

These prophetic words did come to pass, as they later denied receiving the apparitions. Thus, the bishop and his successors had cause for serious reservations about the authenticity of the apparitions. Bishop Fernandez and his immediate successor Bishop Eugenio Beitia issued "Notas." These "Notas" advised caution and restricted priests from visiting the village without permission. They stated further that there was no evidence that any supernatural events had taken place. However, it is significant to note that Bishop Beitia, in his "Notas" of July 8, 1965, stated: *"... We would like to say, however, that we have found no grounds for an ecclesiastical condemnation either in the doctrine or in the spiritual recommendations that have been divulged in the events and addressed to the Christian faithful; furthermore, these recommendations contain exhortations to prayer, sacrifice, devotion to the Holy Eucharist and devotion to the Blessed Virgin under traditional, praiseworthy forms; there are also exhortations to a holy fear of the Lord, offended by our sins…."*

In a letter dated May 7, 2007 the Archbishop of Oviedo, Carlos Osoro Sierra, the Apostolic Administrator of the Diocese of Santander wrote to an American by the name of Edward Kelly. Kelly was an American who married a woman from Garabandal, and then lived in California. The letter was printed in the Garabandal Journal/Special Edition. Bishop Sierra wrote, *"I encourage you to continue maintaining this devotion to Our Mother…. I am open to all information and to every consideration about Garabandal."* From the same publication, there is a letter published in which Msgr. Stanislaus Dziwisz (Cardinal of Krakov Poland) once secretary to John Paul II, responded on behalf of the pope to a book by German author Albrecht Weber he received on Garabandal. *"May God reward you for everything, especially the deep love with which you are making the events connected with Garabandal more widely known. May the message of the Mother of God, find an entrance into hearts before it is too late. As an expression of joy and gratitude, the Holy Father gives you his apostolic blessing."* Accompanying this letter was a greeting by John Paul II in his own handwriting.

Abortion Referenced by Our Lady

Among the many prophecies of Garabandal was one that only came to light with the publication of Weber's book on Garabandal in 1992. Weber was in Garabandal on the day of Conchita's last apparition on November 13, 1965, and had a conversation with the visionary. The following excerpt from his book deals with some of what the visionary told him:

"She (Conchita) spoke quite openly about the developments by which men in the near future would rebel against God. On the day after Our Lady's last appearance at Garabandal, Conchita asked the author, *'Can you imagine how someone could kill children in the womb without thereby killing the mother?'* The author spontaneously answered, *'No, what gave you that idea, Conchita.'* Well, the Blessed Mother spoke about this and she let me know that this will happen with the overflowing of the chalice."* [In the second message of June 18, 1965, the Virgin said, *"Before the cup was filling up. Now it is flowing over."*]

"Conchita said this trembling without being able to visualize what it really implied. She said it disturbed her very much but that she felt ridiculous because she hadn't understood at all how this could happen. The Blessed Virgin had not explained it to her, and up until that moment, nobody had been able to explain it to her at all."

"Conchita would learn soon enough when abortion became legalized, even in her own country."

(This story on abortion above in its entirety is verbatim from the *The Garabandal Journal,* January/February, 2004, page 11).

Possible Data Points on the Timing of the Warning

Pope to Visit Moscow?

As mentioned, German author Albrecht Weber was devoted to Garabandal from the time of the apparitions to his death in 2014. He is buried at Garabandal, and in no way would ever wish to harm what happened there. He devoted his life to making the messages of Garabandal known. Weber is the sole origin of the story that the reigning pope would visit Moscow near the time of the Warning. Weber claimed Conchita told him that when meeting with her at the time of the apparitions in 1965. Pope Francis has expressed interest in visiting Moscow and said so on his way back to Rome after his five-day Greece and Cyprus trip in December 2021. Patriarch Kirill of Moscow then sent a representative soon after to the Vatican to work out details. Pope Francis visited the Russian Embassy on February 25, 2022 in Rome, at the beginning of the Russia Ukraine war, presumably making a plea for peace. It has been nearly 1,000 years since Eastern Orthodoxy split from Rome, so it would be a significant event. However, at the time of this writing, no date has been given for Pope Francis to visit Moscow. What is odd, is that this story had not surfaced until fairly recently about Weber's claim. After multiple decades of speculation when the Warning may take place, this story had not been spoken of or widely disseminated. However, events are now pointing to the fruition of the prophecies by just looking at the social upheaval in the world. If Weber is correct, we will know shortly.

Was the Synod on Synodality the Synod Prophesied at Garabandal?

Another event that is interesting to note on the possible timing of the Warning is that it would be around the time of a synod. Synods are not new in the Church, and there have been many since the apparitions ended in 1965. But a Spanish nun by the name of Mother Nieves Garcia who was the head of Conchita's boarding school in Spain knew Conchita since her school days, said she was told the Warning would be near the time of a Synod. Conchita had allegedly told Mother Nieves that "an important one" {Synod} would be held before the events took place. Pope Francis has initiated a program called *The Synod on Synodality* which is a two-year process of listening and dialogue that began with a solemn opening in Rome on October 9, 10, 2021. The reason it is an *"important one"* is that it has relevance to every diocese and parish in the world because there has never been one quite like it. The Synodal process will conclude in 2023. Pope Francis said about the synod, *"I invite the Church to reflect on the theme that is decisive for its life and mission. It is precisely this path of synodality which God expects the Church of the third millennium. This journey which follows in the wake of the Church's renewal proposed by the Second Vatican Council, is both a gift and a task: by journeying together and reflecting together on the journey that has been made, the Church will be able to learn through her experience which processes can help her to live communion, to active participation to open herself to mission."*

This is another controversy because many people feel that Pope Francis might use the Synod to make changes that will be more progressive than many like, taking the Church in a direction conservatives feel will aid in the further destruction of orthodoxy and tradition. At the diocesan level there are meetings mandated by bishops with clergy participating in listening sessions with laity to discuss the direction of the Church. Conservatives are concerned that it will bring more of a liberal social justice agenda to these "listening sessions" throughout the world.

The Issue of the Number of Popes

After Pope John XXIII died, Conchita said that Our Lady told her, *"After this pope there will be only three left, but there would be a fourth pope who would govern the Church for a short time, then it would be the end of times."*

This gets into a highly controversial matter as to the issue of when she said this. It is alleged there was pressure from Conchita's mother on releasing this portion of the message relating to the reign of a pope for just a short time to not create controversy for her daughter. Since John XXIII, we have had Paul VI, John Paul I, then John Paul II, Benedict XVI, and now Pope Francis. We do know that John Paul I governed only thirty-three days, which is an amazingly accurate prophecy in light of that fact it did happen. If the above is true, then that would mean the conclave electing Pope Francis ushered in the end times. It is a plausible scenario but still controversial. Initially Conchita indicated there would be only three popes before "the end times," **a New Era of humanity, not the end of the world.**

The Role of Communism is Still a Dominant Theme that Never Seems to go Away

A Mrs. Christine Bocabeille asked Mary Loli, *"since you are not allowed to tell me the exact year of the Warning, perhaps you could tell me approximately when it will happen?* Loli responded, *"it will be at a time when the world will most need it."* Then it was asked when is that? Loli said, **When Russia will suddenly and unexpectedly overrun a great part of the free world.** *God does not want this to happen so quickly. In any case the Warning will come when you will see the Holy Mass cannot be celebrated freely anymore; then it will be that the world will most need the intervention of God."*

Mari-Loli did not know the date/day of the Warning, only the year. Conchita alone knows the day of the Miracle. Mari-Loli also said that the Blessed Mother told her prior to the Warning and the Great Miracle, *"A time would come, when it would look like the Church was finished, when priests would have difficulty saying Mass and talking about holy things. There would come a time when the Church would give the impression of being on the point of perishing. It would pass through a terrible test. Priests would supposedly have to hide in order to say Mass. It is then that the world will be in most need of God's intervention."* When she asked Our Lady how this would happen, Our Lady called it *"**communism**.* This has happened in many countries already. Whether or not it will be more widespread remains to be seen.

It is much easier to manipulate and control an individual that does not acknowledge the truth of Christianity, which is precisely why it must be removed by a tyrannical government. We have seen the brutality of communist regimes from the USSR and China and other brute dictators, but communism is simply a government where God cannot be publicly displayed. Through sophisticated social engineering, much of the west, and the world at large, exhibit a form of theoretical and practical atheism — or communism as it comes to everyday living. A world without God is the communist (global elite) goal.

The Blessed Mother once told Conchita, *"**it would be like an invasion of Communism.**"* Premier Mikhail Gorbachev said the event that toppled the USSR was the nuclear disaster at Chernobyl April 26, 1986. The ramifications of

Soviet incompetence spreading throughout western borders was no longer acceptable to the West, and Gorbachev was firm when he said it was this event that led to the 1992-1994 downfall. As the world watches the destruction of the Ukraine and the issues that it is causing world-wide, one would have to ask, has communism really fallen?

The girls described the times of tribulation as *"the return of Communism."* Four young mountain children in the early 1960's would not have any understanding of what Communism meant. In political philosophy Communism does not necessarily have to be violent, although it usually is. Communism is an ideological practice without God in the governance of the state. Due to theoretical and practical atheism globally, we increasingly see a world that does not want God in any genre or milieu of life. Many classrooms across the world continue to be cesspools with a lack of any moral formation, with many countries outright reverting to paganism. This would constitute Communism returning on a much wider scale than what we have seen in the past.

Prelude to The Warning or
The Illumination of Conscience

Believers who know the messages of Garabandal have been waiting in joyful hope many years for the events prophesied at Garabandal to come to pass soon. There has been a parlor game for decades trying to match data points to come up with plausible dates for the Miracle. To date, none have been correct as terms and conditions have not yet been fulfilled. But, one thing is certain, with the speed of events in an interconnected world, things can happen quickly.

People anxiously await these events because in the interior of their souls, it is only going to be through this enormous grace of the Warning and the Miracle that Heaven has promised the world, that our culture can turn away from such a reprobate moral state. It is for this reason so many people follow the movements of Garabandal with expectation and hope. The Warning is God's Ultimate Act of Mercy to mankind.

Our Lady's messages promised three events at Garabandal; a fourth is contingent upon the world's response. The first event will be a world-wide warning from God, known as The Warning. Conchita wrote in a letter on January 1, 1965: *"Our Lady said that a warning would be given to the entire world before the Miracle in order that the world might amend itself. It will come directly from God and be visible throughout the entire world."*

There will be two events to happen *within* one year. The operative word is "**within**." It may be less, but it will not be more than one year from the Warning to the Great Miracle. The word "**within**" doesn't mean it "has to" happen in the same calendar year.

Pope Paul VI (Papacy from 1963-1978) called the struggle of good and evil going on in the world "apocalyptic." Pope Paul quoted Luke 18:8: *"when the Son of Man returns will He find faith on earth,"* and said the *"smoke of Satan had entered the sanctuary."* The Blessed Mother also said at

Fatima, **"In the end my Immaculate Heart will Triumph."** The Triumph of her Immaculate Heart is the return of Jesus in glory. As the Blessed Mother said at Cana instructing the servants, *"Do whatever He tells you"* (John 2:5). The Holy Trinity has appointed her for this task specifically at this point in time. If one thing is gleaned from this entire narrative, it is this; *The refuge is her Immaculate Heart.* Looking for safety anywhere else will be of limited value and duration. Not taking away from the authority of Jesus in the least, she glorifies His Sacred Heart. She is a co-redeemer with us in His salvation plan for mankind, and what better vessel than His mother who came into the world without the stain of sin through the Immaculate Conception!

The messages of the Blessed Mother at authentic apparition sites are always clear and direct. They speak in clear language about the basic tenets of the faith. Not philosophy or theology few can understand, but Our Lady's messages always go to the heart of what is true and good. When a life changing experience or a message is heard and absorbed, there is a transformation of the soul. Pope Paul VI, Saint John Paul II, Father Stefano Gobbi of the Marian Movement of Priests, and many other contemporaries of our time believed in what was said at Garabandal, and were all public in affirming it. Saint Pio (Padre Pio) and St. Teresa of Calcutta also believed in the validity of Garabandal. Both visited with Conchita and extended their blessings and prayers to her. Saint Pio on the occasion of his visit with her, took Conchita's hand and her crucifix that

Our Lady had kissed and held them both. The crucifix had been passed through the hands of the child Jesus during the apparition of November 13, 1965.

However, what made Garabandal unique, is that the girls spoke about two events that would happen that have been spoken about by other mystics in the church like Saint Edmund Campion, and Blessed Anna Maria Taigi. Other more contemporary mystics like Servant of God Maria Esperanza of Betania/Caracas, Venezuela have addressed the same subjects.

The Warning is where each person will see the state of his or her soul as God would judge it upon death. It will be a line of demarcation in all of history. Satan's lie will be exposed for who he is, and he will know we know it. His grip will be loosened. There will still be sin in the world after the event. The free will of man will still be present, but the neutrality of people will be gone. You will either be for the things of God, or not. As the Jews wandered in the desert after they left the four hundred years of captivity in Egypt, it was not long before they forgot what God had done for them. Shortly thereafter, they were making a golden calf in the desert. Manna and quail were falling from the sky to feed the migratory people heading to the promised land, and they were soon offering up a pagan rite. It will be the same today. People will soon forget the graces they have been given during *"The Warning,"* and go back to old ways because they have not been properly formed in the faith. It is for this reason formation in the faith is so important. *"Faith comes by hearing, hearing by the Word,"* (Romans

10:17), and as the Psalmist said, *"I have hid the word of God in my heart that I may not sin against thee"* (Ps. 119:11).

There are several events that indicate the Warning **may** be getting closer. The issue of Pope Francis going to Moscow is one. If not Pope Francis, maybe the next. The prophecy that a time would come when the Mass will be suppressed, and priests will go into hiding. There are places in the world where priests are persecuted and worse. At the time of the apparitions in Garabandal, Vatican II was simultaneously taking place. All know the Mass did change after Vatican II. There are people who attend the Traditional Latin Mass (TLM) today who feel that this prophecy may have taken place as the TLM has been suppressed, thus fulfilled. It seems as if there may be two separate issues. One is suppression and the other is much more serious with priests having difficulty saying the Mass and have to go in hiding. It would logically seem that going into hiding is serious social unrest.

Two Key Messages of Garabandal

Our Lady revealed the first message for the world. She told the girls to announce the message publicly on October 18, 1961. On this day, the children made known the message: *"Many sacrifices must be made, much penance must be done.* **We must pay many visits to the Blessed Sacrament...but first of all we must be very good ...if we do not do this, punishment awaits us...already the cup is** *filling, and if we do not change, we will be punished."* That message given to the young girls was heavily centered on conversion and amendment of life. The Blessed Mother had a continual theme as to the urgency of our times and what would happen, IF man did not repent.

The message continued: *"If you ask pardon with a sincere soul, He will pardon you. It is I your Mother, who through the intercession of Saint Michael, wish to say that you amend, that you are already in the last warnings and that I love you much and do not want your condemnation. Ask us sincerely and we will give to you. You should sacrifice more. Think of the Passion of Jesus."* **Our Lady appeared wearing the Brown Scapular, an indication we should wear it, and taught the children how to pray the rosary. Her greatest emphasis was placed on the Eucharist and prayers for the priests.**

On January 1, 1965, the Blessed Virgin told Conchita that the Archangel Michael would appear to her on the following June 18th to deliver a final message in Mary's name for the entire world, because her first message was not heeded. Saint Michael appeared to Conchita while she was in ecstasy, which lasted approximately sixteen minutes. On June 18, 1965 the following message was delivered to the world: *"As my message of October 18th [1961] has not been complied with and has not been made known to the world, I am advising you that this is the last one. Before the cup was filling up. Now it is flowing over. Many cardinals, many bishops, and many priests are on the road to perdition and are taking many souls with them. Less and less importance is being given to the Eucharist.*

"You should turn the wrath of God away from yourselves by your efforts. If you ask His forgiveness with sincere hearts, He will pardon you. I, your mother, through the intercession of Saint Michael the Archangel, ask you to amend your lives. You are now receiving the last warning. I love you very much and do not want your condemnation. Pray to Us with sincerity and We will grant your requests. You should make more sacrifices. Think about the passion of Jesus."

There are several very important things contained in that message. First and foremost, beyond temporal concerns, is **the importance of the Eucharist and Adoration.** It states clearly if people do not change, there will be punishment. Also, some clergy are leading souls to perdition. But, not just priests, but bishops and cardinals. These are profound statements with broad implications for the Church, the family, and the culture. It would be wise to reflect on these two messages and what they mean for us today. At the time that message was issued, the challenges to Church teaching with the sexual scandal involving priests had not fully unfolded.

The last apparition for Conchita was on November 13, 1965 at the Pines. Conchita described this last conversation as happy, but Our Lady gently chastised her: *"Conchita, why don't you go often to visit my Son in the Most Blessed Sacrament?"*

Often, people who speak today on such subjects like this in public will frequently be ridiculed. You will hear this is an Old Testament mentality on the wrathful God. This was said in the 1960's and it is not some Old Testament prophet shouting it from the rooftops. A decision must be made on our theology and our perception of who God is in our life, and come to a realization that not all is well in the world — and Heaven has a plan. It comes to one major issue: This is Heaven's agenda, we are to embrace and declare it. Living the Gospel is being asked of us. Often the more conservative element in the church, focus excessively on doctrine and are critical of what the Blessed Mother is doing in the world. They will venerate and pay lip service to her titles in Heaven, but if she speaks, they can't run fast enough to get away, not wanting to be associated with it. They often forget that the gospel is about people, and fallen people at that. The more liberal groups will often dismiss it as an outdated theology for a modern world.

More often than not, they have their own agendas which usually focus on social justice to the exclusion of nearly everything else. A feel good 'luving" church. Luv everywhere, luv everyone, with few boundaries on behavior, making up new theology along the way as they consider the Church outdated. Both sides fail to see the essential issue is to do what the Holy Spirit is asking. In addition, often the Marian devotee focuses so much on the severe parts of the messages of the Blessed Mother, they see nothing but doom and gloom to the exclusion of everything else, and forget that the gospel means, *"The Good News."* There has been great fruit from many of apparition sites throughout the world over the centuries bringing people to a deeper faith.

In Revelation 2 and 3, the Holy Spirit speaks to the seven churches that will have different spirits and charisms throughout millennia. Each of the churches has a major strength. No church has it all together except the Church of Philadelphia (Rev. 3: 7-13) as it is the only church the Lord does not find fault, because it embraces love. Each of the others, it is said, *"and this I have against you"*…, but Philadelphia. This is where we need to arrive. We need to be transformed to arrive at neither left nor right in our theology and philosophy, but through finding peace of soul by living the gospel, where we are to love unconditionally. Our service will come because of our love and obedience to Scripture, and the Magisterium of the Church. Social Justice needs to be rooted in what we hear in prayer and fidelity to the laws of God, not a godless leftist political agenda creating havoc in the streets.

The Transition of Civilization Takes Place, Two Events to Come — the First Will be the Warning

The first of two events will be a world-wide warning from God. Conchita wrote in a letter dated on January 1, 1965 where she said, *"Our Lady said that a Warning would be given to the entire world before the Miracle in order that the world might amend itself. It will come directly from God and be visible throughout the entire world."* Conchita wrote on June 2, 1965, *"The warning, like the chastisement is a fearful thing for the good as well as the wicked. It will draw the good closer to God and warn the wicked the end of times is coming. These are the last warnings."* Conchita explained *"that the warning is a purification to prepare us for the miracle. Each person on earth will have an interior experience of how he or she stands in the light of God's Justice. Believers and nonbelievers alike will experience the Warning."* Those living in a state of grace will have less severe impact from it we are also told by other mystics. Mari Loli Mazon who lived in Massachusetts before she died in 2009, was the only visionary to know the year of the Warning, but not the day of the Great Miracle. Mari Loli said, *"We will see it and feel it within ourselves, and it will be most clear that it comes from God."*

Jacinta Gonzalez said: *"The Warning is something that is first seen in the air, everywhere in the world and immediately is transmitted into the interior of our souls. It will last for a very little time, but it will seem a very long time because of its effect within us. It will be for the good of our souls, in order to see in ourselves our conscience... the good that we have failed to do, and the bad that we have done. Then we will feel a great love towards our heavenly Parents and ask forgiveness for all our offenses. The Warning is for everybody because God wants our salvation. The Warning is for us to draw closer to Him and to increase our faith. Therefore, one should prepare for that day, but not await it with fear. God does not send things for the sake of fear but rather with justice and love. He does it for the good of all His children so they might enjoy eternal happiness and not be lost."*

Are We Close to the Warning?

How much closer to this year of the Warning could we be? At this point in America, leading political figures are far more communist than socialist. Closer to Stalinist is actually more accurate where many leaders wish to bring western countries. Worldwide, America has lagged other countries in implementing communist principles, but now she seems eager to catch up. Many are promoting a communist ideology demanding faith be removed from the culture in every way possible. If a politician won't say it, they will often try to legislate it into reality, while they personally benefit from the largesse a capitalist structure affords them to live. The *"invasion of Communism"* is gaining ground in the USA faster than at any time since the Great Depression of the 1930s. A world that submerges into moral relativism where sin does not exist, fits a cleaner definition of communism. Today we have people who do not obey the commandments of God, yet will attend church paying more attention to cultural and state norms than Biblical truth. In essence, a state run, politically acceptable faith void of God, is increasingly the situation in the U.S. Language engineering and social manipulation are key to controlling the populace, and maintaining a godless narrative. We are seeing Our Lady's prophecy on communism being fulfilled with state control of all social structures. Inch by inch this goal has been achieved over several generations. Taking the Bible and prayer out of the classroom by order of the U.S. Supreme Court in America was a significant step with this agenda.

The Warning is Worldwide

Father Joseph Pelletier, the late Marian scholar and author (1912-1986 and Professor at Assumption College), asked Conchita several questions and offered further insight about the events of Garabandal. Conchita's answer on June 19, 1965, is as follows: *"Here in writing is the Warning that the Blessed Virgin gave me when I was alone at the pines on January 1ˢᵗ of this year, 1965. The Warning that the Blessed Virgin will give us is like a chastisement. Its purpose is to draw the good nearer to God and to warn the others. I cannot reveal what the Warning will consist of. The Blessed Virgin did not tell me to announce it. Nothing further. God would like that through this warning, we amend our lives and that we commit less sins against Him."* To the question posed by Marian and Garabandal scholar Father Laffineur whether the Warning would cause death, Conchita said, *"If we die from it, it would not be from the Warning itself, but from the emotional shock that we would experience in seeing and feeling the Warning."*

Statements were made by Conchita in response to questions put to her:

Q. Will the Warning be a visible thing or an interior thing or both?

A. **The Warning is a thing that comes directly from God. It will be visible all over the world, in whatever place anyone might be.**

Q. Will the Warning reveal his personal sins to every
   person in the world and to persons of all faiths, including
   atheists.

A. *Yes, the Warning will be like the revelation of our sins,
   and it will be seen and felt equally by believers and non-
   believers, and people of any religion whatsoever.*

In reply to a question whether the Warning might be a
comet that was approaching the Earth, Conchita said: *"I
don't know what a comet is. If it is something that depends
on man's will, I answer — no. If it is something that God will
do, it is quite possible."* When the woman expressed fear,
the latter replied: *"Oh, yes, the Warning will be very fearful,
a thousand times worse than earthquakes."* To an inquiry
concerning the nature of the Warning, Conchita answered:
**"It will be like fire. It will not burn our flesh, but we will
feel it bodily and interiorly."** She added, *"We shall comment
on this later. All nations and all persons will experience it in
the same way. No one will escape it. Even the nonbelievers
themselves will experience the fear of God. Even if you hide
in your room and close the blinds, you will not escape it. You
will feel and see it just the same. Yes, it is true. The Blessed
Virgin gave me the name of the phenomenon. It begins with
an 'A.' but she did not tell me to reveal it to anyone."*

As the lady again expressed her fear, Conchita added:
*"Oh, but after the Warning, you will love the good Lord very
much."* To the question: *"What about the Miracle?"* she said,
"The Miracle will not delay in coming." Conchita added an
interesting observation: *"Although it is taking time to come,
it will not be late. God's time is always the appropriate time."*

An important note should be added: when Conchita describes the Warning as being *"like fire,"* she means that in some way or ways it resembles fire but that it is not fire. According to Conchita, the Warning and fire have two things in common: *"they can be seen and felt, and they are very terrifying. The Warning will be seen and felt by all men and will cause great fear in men's hearts, a fear so great that it could conceivably cause some to die. To want a precise and detailed description of the phenomenon in human terms is to seek the impossible. Also, it is not necessary. This should be enough to prompt us to* **take measures now so as to be ready for the Warning when it comes.**"

Fatima and the Illumination of Conscience

The **Warning / Illumination of Conscience / Life Review / Judgment in Miniature** is a worldwide event where everyone in the world will see the state of their soul as God would judge them based upon the life they have lived. It brings one's thinking to the The Four Last Things: DEATH, JUDGMENT, HEAVEN, HELL. We will know that it is God communicating in absolute love, and there will be no rebuttal. There will be no exceptions to this. After speaking to numerous people over the last thirty years who have experienced a near-death experience (NDE), I have learned it often takes them years to emotionally and intellectually sort it out and put the event into words. The Warning will be more profound than a near death experience. There are parallels between Fatima and Garabandal.

Something that is seldom if ever spoken of is that Lucia, Francisco, and Jacinta at Fatima described something similar: seeing oneself in the Divine Light of Truth. On the very first apparition of May 13, 1917, Our Lady revealed Divine Mysteries in an aura of light exactly how the visionaries of Garabandal speak of it. Lucia wrote, *"we were able to see ourselves in God, Who was this Light, more clearly than we see ourselves in the best of mirrors."* All three of the children witnessed themselves as God would see them, and more importantly, what God was asking of them. This would make sense as the Lord would want to reinforce to the visionaries what He says will happen — did happen. This would also reinforce their belief they were not being deceived, and would have the strength to go forward and continue their mission in spite of obstacles. It enables one to minimize doubt going forward.

Just two months later on July 13, 1917, all three witnessed a vision of Hell. The impact that this would have on nine-year old Francisco Marto (9 is very young) is hard to imagine. Heaven decided it would be beneficial for these very young children to see Hell. Today, if one were to speak of Hell, many would consider it extreme or even cruel to a child as the faith has become so sanitized. Yet, Heaven thought otherwise in 1917. Up until his premature death of the Spanish flu on April 4, 1919, Francisco spent his remaining time praying the Rosary, consoling God for the sins of mankind. He would often make visits to the Blessed Sacrament to see *"the Hidden Jesus."* Everyone in the Marto family died from the Spanish flu with the exception of his father.

Why this fact is so seldom spoken about Fatima is puzzling. It can validate other apparitions where there are similar events. One can see consistencies if there is a cumulative knowledge of what happens when the Blessed Mother appears.

Another voice weighing in mystically concerning a worldwide event of great magnitude was Pius IX (Pope from 1846-1878) when he said, *"There will come a great sign which will fill the world with awe. But this will occur only after the triumph of a revolution during which the Church will undergo ordeals that are beyond description."*

Father Joseph Brennan, O.C.S., an early writer on Garabandal, summarized the prophetic statements made by saints, blessed and popes. He put it this way: *"They foretell a time of unprecedented and terrible confusion and suffering unlike anything that has ever been experienced in human history. It will affect every area of human life."*

The turbulence of our times is like birth pangs for an expectant mother. The difficult times are increasing like birth pangs, in intensity and severity.

Saint Paul never saw or followed Jesus as one of the original twelve apostles, yet he was the single most important person to promote the Gospel to the world traveling city to city after the Resurrection of Jesus. A thorough knowledge of Scripture enables one to follow the Lord's statutes, precepts, and commands. Having a cumulative knowledge of the Blessed Mother's instructions for mankind enables an individual to have a more acute and deeper understanding of our times. She is a gift, and the gift is only understood in humility and littleness absent of self and ego. Self-abandonment to Divine Providence is key.

In Isaiah, this is exactly what the Lord is saying. Isaiah writes, *"I come to gather nations of every language; they shall come and see my glory.* **I will set a sign among them;** *from them I will send fugitives to the nations…, to the distant coastlands that have never heard of my fame, or seen my glory; and they shall proclaim my glory among the nations. They shall bring all your brethren from all the nations as an offering to the Lord…."* This is clearly talking about the coming of a Messiah and the signs that He would make available to all the nations.

Isaiah continues what it would be like. *"As the new heavens and a new earth which I will make shall endure before me, says the Lord, so shall your name and your race endure. From one new moon to another, and from one Sabbath to another, all mankind shall come to worship before me, says the Lord"* (Is. 66:18-23).

This sign is one of supernatural deliverance and a situation where there is no answer unless it is by the hand of Almighty God Himself. The mission of Jesus is being described in this passage. The memorial of His sign is a testament to what He says will happen for His glory, and the benefit of his people. God speaks through signs to show His people He can be trusted, and what He says will happen. Could the Permanent Sign at Garabandal speak to the Jewish people and bring about the conversion foretold of Jews by St. Paul?

The Warning in Perspective

Our Lady herself explained the warning to Conchita. As Conchita explains it after receiving her last apparition: *"The Blessed Virgin Mary told me before that Jesus does not want to send the punishment in order to distress us but in order to help us and reproach us because we pay no attention to Him.* **And the Warning will be sent in order to purify us for the Miracle in which He will show us His great love,** and in *order that we may fulfill the message."*

Fear of God is a good thing, as Holy Scripture tells us, but the fear of God that is good is not the kind of fear that obsesses us, causes us to worry constantly, and ultimately robs us of our peace of mind and heart, and leads us away from God. The fear of God that is good is the fear that draws virtuous souls to God and prompts sinners to amend their lives. The fear of the Lord translates to **"awesome majesty"** of God. This is precisely the purpose that Conchita ascribed to the Warning. It will cause a holy respect for God. Our concern at this moment should be to get closer to God, casting all sin from our lives and striving to love and serve Him better. If we do this, we will be ready for the Warning when it comes. To be sure, it will strike fear in our hearts. However, this fear will not kill us. It will bring us closer to God because we fear offending Him as a son fears offending his father who is always good to him.

The Great Miracle at the Nine Pines in Garabandal

- The second event Our Lady promised is a **Great Miracle** that will take place above the Pines.

- It will occur on a Thursday evening, at 8:30 PM Spanish time.

- Between the 8th and 16th of March, April, May, or June.

- Much of the literature mentions March, April, or May, but Conchita on television in Ireland once said, March, April, May, or June.

- According to Mari-Loli, the Miracle will take place **WITHIN ONE YEAR AFTER THE WARNING.**

- The **Miracle** will coincide with an important event in the Church.

- It will be on the feast day of a young martyr of the Eucharist.

- It will last about fifteen minutes.

- It will be seen in the sky. It will be possible to photograph and televise this event, but not touch it.

- All those in the village or in the surrounding mountains will see it.

- The sick who are present will **ALL** be cured.

- It will be **THE** greatest Miracle ever performed by Jesus for the world.

The word used here is the definite article **THE**. Ponder for a moment that word and what it may mean. There has been widespread speculation on **exactly** what the Grand Milagro may be, however, we only have cryptic messages of exactly what it may be.

- Sinners and non-believers will be converted. The incredulous will believe.

- Russia will be converted after the Miracle.

- Conchita, who knows the date of the Great Miracle, will announce it eight days in advance.

- Conchita tells us that the reigning Pope will see the Miracle from wherever he is.

Conchita said about this great supernatural event:

1. Before the Miracle there will be many reported "apparitions" throughout the world. She said this in December, 1962.
2. A Bishop of Santander will come along who will not believe at first but will receive a sign and allow priests to go to Garabandal for the Miracle.
3. Before the Miracle many will stop believing in Garabandal.

Based upon compiled data over a lifetime, I think the **Great Miracle** will be so extraordinary, with millions making the journey to Garabandal, it will be as the miracles the Hebrews saw leaving Egypt after 400 years of captivity. The Miracle will be an undeniable act of God. The parting of the Red Sea by Moses was a significant event by any standard of miracles in the Bible, but that was a local event where a finite number of people witnessed it. Not to dimmish the parting of the Red Sea by any means! The Warning will be an event every person in the world will witness, and the Permanent Sign after the Great Miracle at Garabandal can be seen by anyone who wishes to journey there to see it. The more details of the Garabandal story are read and digested, the more it is difficult to process all of the phenomena that happened from 1961-1965. But, when millions recount the same stories of miraculous warnings, their witness will validate its legitimacy to the most hardened skeptic. People will fall on their knees in repentance when the promised Miracle is seen from the natural amphitheater of the tranquil Cantabrian Mountains looking down upon the nine pines. That in itself is part of a much bigger story that is being scripted by Heaven. The sins of man are so great and solutions so elusive, it will take an event such as this to reorient man to God's design for living.

The Little Miracle — A Visible Host

The time the Eucharist miraculously was placed on Conchita's tongue by St. Michael, was called by her the "Little Miracle," and it became visible for all to see. The miracle of the visible Host for Conchita occurred at 1:40

a.m. on July 19, 1962. Hundreds of witnesses were present. The event was recorded on film by a businessman from Barcelona. This film was later submitted to the bishop of Santander. Witnesses said that Conchita knelt and put out her tongue to receive the Host. At first, nothing was visible. In a few moments, a white Host, thicker than usual, appeared on her tongue. It remained there for a few moments before being consumed. This *"little miracle"* was chosen to call our attention to the reality of the Real Presence of Our Lord in the Holy Eucharist.

The reception by Conchita of the Eucharist is a major part of the story of Garabandal. This mystical Communion of Conchita significantly highlights the main focus of the entire four years of apparitions is the **importance of the Eucharist and priesthood to the faith.** Even bilocation is more common than a mystical Communion given by an angel.

The Great Miracle Will be Eucharistic and Marian

Could the *"little miracle"* of Conchita receiving the Eucharist be the precursor to a bigger Eucharistic event?

The Miracle will be Eucharistic. The emphasis on devotion to the Most Holy Eucharist is so strong at Garabandal that a Eucharistic theme for the Miracle would be in perfect consonance with everything that happened in the village during the apparitions.

The Miracle will be ecclesial, that is, it will support the truth that through the Body of Christ, which is the Church, all graces come, and that all men and women are called not only to follow Jesus personally, but also to enter His Church and to submit to its discipline, teaching, and sacraments. For this reason, the Miracle will happen in connection with a great ecclesiastical event, and the Church's authority will be reinforced and authenticated by the fact of the *"ecclesiastical event."*

The Miracle will be Marian. It will assert the glory of the Mother of God, so that all Christians will give up their objections to her role in the Body of Christ and pay her the honor that God Himself gives her. The world will begin to give the Immaculate Heart of Mary the honor and devotion due her. Through this great miracle, many will begin to love *"Holy Mary, Mother of God."*

The Miracle is for the conversion of the whole world. This assertion was made by Our Lord Himself to Conchita at Garabandal. The Lord answered her question about Russia's conversion by assuring her that *"the Miracle was not only for the conversion of Russia,"* but *"for the conversion of the whole world,"* and that **"thus, all will love Our Hearts"** (the Hearts of Jesus and Mary).

It seems by His words that somehow **the Miracle will show us all how closely the Hearts of Jesus and Mary are united,** as a symbol of the peace-giving love that should unite our hearts. Perhaps the Two Hearts on the reverse side of the "Miraculous Medal" were a prophecy as well as a lesson. Reconciliation of hearts is what conversion is all about, and it seems that all authentic Marian appearances concern themselves with that message.

Unless the people heed the message of the Miracle, the punishment will come. There will be no escape from it. The Warning will set the fuse as we know the Miracle is within one year from the Warning.

Martyrs of the Eucharist — One Stands Out

A parlor game for decades has been to guess who is the *"little known martyr of the Eucharist"*, as the Miracle will happen on this individual's feast day. The Miracle is supposed to happen on a prescribed day, on a certain month and time, and on a Thursday. Many have thought it may be Saint Hermenegild of Spain whose feast day is April 13, and is a martyr who died in the year 586. Others have thought a good candidate, and validly so, is Saint Pancras (died circa 304 or 305AD), also a martyr at the age of fourteen with a feast day on May 12th.

But there is one little girl who falls in line with the mystical of the Eucharist like no other, and her name is seldom mentioned. Her named is **Blessed Imelda Lambertini.** She was born in Bologna, Italy in 1322. Imelda begged to receive the Eucharist at the age of nine and was denied because she was too young. One day at Mass the Eucharist was suspended in pure light and she was able to receive Our Lord without the aid of a priest. Imelda went back to her seat and died of ecstasy and pure joy. She was beatified in 1826 and is considered to be a Patron Saint of First Communicants.

Imelda died on May 12th, but her feast day is celebrated on May 13th. What is fascinating and rare by all accounts for mysticism in the Catholic Church is the extremely infrequent mystical appearance and reception of the Host. In the case of Conchita, she mystically received a Host on her tongue from Saint Michael, and for Imelda, the Host mystically appeared on her tongue as well. Blessed Imelda, a little-known saint of the Mystical Eucharist, fits all the criteria and framework of the spirit of the apparitions at Garabandal.

The Old Testament and Garabandal

If one were to be dropped to the Earth from outer space and had never read or known anything about the Bible, and read only the Old Testament (the Hebrew Scriptures to the Jewish people) one would ask where is the rest of this book? The people and the events of the Old Testament point to events predicted to happen in the future, that happened exactly as the Hebrew Scriptures said they would. Similarly, if that person just read the New Testament, there are many stories that speak of people named Jonah, Joel, David, Joshua, Noah, Moses, Elijah, and others, that refer to the first half of the book, because the Bible is broken up into two distinct parts — before the birth of Jesus Christ and after.

When the two testaments are read in their entirety, the New validates the Old, and vice versa. When one studies the Old and the New, there is an understanding of what God is asking of us. There is a completeness and fullness in the New that was prophesied in the Old. Jesus said, *"I did not come to abolish the law, but to fulfill it"* (Matt. 5:17). What messages might the New bring to the Old? Romans 9:4-5 speaks about the privileges of Israel. It reads: *"They were adopted as sons, they were given the glory and the covenants; the Law and the ritual were drawn up for them, and the promises were made to them. They are descended from the patriarchs and from their flesh and blood came Christ who is above all, God forever blessed!"* In Romans 11:26, St. Paul also foretells that *"all Israel should be saved, as it is written: there shall come out of Zion he that shall deliver, and shall turn away godlessness from Jacob."* The apparitions and messages of Garabandal are overflowing with Old Testament signs as part of Heaven's plan for the conversion of the world and a new Era of Peace, a New Jerusalem — New Times — which Heaven has promised.

I am a Jewess in Heaven

Conchita described Mary in her diary as a beautiful Jewish woman with dark and wavy hair, a perfect nose, full lips, and a rather dark complexion. In other apparitions Mary appears as a beautiful girl with the features of other beautiful girls of the country where she appears. Mari-Loli asked her one day if she was Jewish, and her answer was yes, and she said she was a Jewess in Heaven. It was the first time in the history of apparitions that the Blessed Virgin identified herself as such, saying that even in Heaven she belonged to the Jewish people. This was confirmed by the late Garabandal writer Father Laffineur.

Mt. Carmel

For the first time in the history of Marian apparitions, as announced by St. Michael, the Blessed Mother appeared under a title that refers to a Biblical holy place — Mount Carmel. The three holy mountains of the ancient people of Israel were Mount Carmel, Mount Sinai or Horeb, and Mount Zion or Jerusalem. Mount Carmel is the mountain made holy by Elijah the prophet. It is the mountain which Mary could see from where she lived in the village of Nazareth. Moreover, of all religious orders, the Carmelites are by far the closest to Judaism. Elijah is considered by Carmelite friars and sisters as their founder and model.

St. Michael the Archangel

A great deal has been written on St. Michael's role at Garabandal. St. Michael was the forerunner of Mary and her messenger to Conchita on several occasions. Might his appearance also have significance for the Jewish people? St. Michael is named three times in the Old Testament, each time as a guardian of Israel or as its Prince. Daniel 10:20 reads: *"He said then, 'Do you know why I have come to you? It is to tell you what is written in the Book of Truth. I must go back to fight against the prince of Persia: when I have done with him, the prince of Javan will come next. In all this there is no one to lend me support except Michael your prince.'"*

Daniel 12: 1-4 describes Michael again and his role in the latter times: *"At that time Michael will stand up, the great prince who mounts guard over your people. There is going to be a time of great distress, unparalleled since nations first came into existence. When that time comes, your own people will be spared, all those whose names are found written in the Book.... But you, Daniel, must keep your words secret and the book sealed until the time of the end. Many will wander this way and that, and wickedness will go on increasing."* Michael will *"stand up in a time of great trouble,"* and thanks to him *"thy people shall be spared."*

Daniel 10:13 tells about the apparition of Michael: *"The prince of the kingdom of Persia has been resisting me for twenty-one days, but Michael, one of the leading princes, came to my assistance."* His power is great as he is *"one of the leading princes."* Although the Church applies this passage to itself, it is not possible to exclude *"those who are Israelites,*" as they were the first to have Michael as their prince.

As Isaiah and others clearly pointed to the birth of a Messiah, Garabandal is pointing to something the world has never seen before. Those with a knowledge of Isaiah before the birth of Christ, were able to see the fulfillment of his prophesies. Jesus quoted Isaiah more than any other prophet for good reason — Isaiah was clear on who Jesus was, and what He would do — His mission. Only at the Lord's death did it all make sense. All things were fulfilled to the letter, exactly as it had been written by many in the Hebrew Scriptures with the birth of the Savior. Garabandal will make more sense after the events — and the events will validate what the Blessed Mother said in the early 1960s. It will be similar to what Isaiah prophesied about the coming of the Messiah, which happened exactly as was written.

The Blessed Mother is the prophetess of our age appointed by the Most Holy Trinity interceding for mankind. This is similar in the same way Queen Esther interceded to the Persian King Ahasuerus to save her people from destruction. Esther prayed and fasted for three days before meeting with the king. Approaching the king unannounced could have cost Queen Esther her life, yet she had the confidence and boldness to intercede for her people. As Queen Esther interceded to save her people, the Blessed Mother never ceases to be an advocate for all mankind. She acts as any mother would. Queen Esther is a precursor to the Blessed Mother's role interceding to the Most Holy Trinity for all mankind.

Is the Permanent Sign a Message to the Jews?

Conchita was told by the Blessed Virgin that a sign would remain at the Pines and it would remain there forever. It would be possible to photograph and televise it, but not touch it. It would appear as a thing not of this world, but it would originate from God. It would be miraculous, a permanent miracle. Is it comparable to a pillar of smoke, but also to rays of sunlight, insofar as it can be seen but not touched? It will be made up of an unknown substance. All the Hebrews who followed Moses out of Egypt saw the *"pillar of cloud by day and of fire by night"* (Exodus 13:21), saving them from the Egyptians (Exodus 14:24), accompanying the Torah at Mount Sinai (Exodus 19: 16-18,34 :5), remaining present among His people, serving as their guide *"wherever they halted on their journey,"* (Exodus 40:36), *"marking out their encampments"* (Deuteronomy 1:33). **The prophets announced it would come back, "a cloud and smoke by day, and the shining of a flaming fire by night"** (Isaiah 4:5). *"It shall come to pass that I will pour out my spirit upon everyone... and I will show wonders in the heavens and on Earth, blood, fire, and pillars of smoke"* (Joel 2: 30).

The luminous cloud has always been a choice subject of rabbinic thought and of Christian mystical theology. All Jews know what the pillar meant: a manifestation of God dwelling among His chosen people, tabernacling amongst them, guiding them, shedding light upon them, speaking to them. The other nations knew this (Numbers 14: 14). It is the Shekinah, the most sacred and mysterious sign of the deity. The Shekinah Glory is Heaven itself. It is God's physical presence that was with the Ark of the Covenant in the desert. A cloud by day, a fire by night.

Conchita has said that the Permanent Sign will be like a pillar of smoke above the pines. **On November 18, 1961, a column of smoke by day and fire by night was seen by a number of people between the nine pines.** Ramon Gonzalez, a shepherd about twenty years old, was tending his sheep and noticed a small fire about 50 centimeters in diameter. Again, in the Autumn 1962, this was seen by a number of people for a period of two or three months, all of whom provided written testimony. It was seen again on November 25, 1965, by four French witnesses. The column was seen at night, clear and luminous. The significance of this is hard to explain to the uninformed. This is just one event of the four years of mystical phenomena that surrounded Garabandal from 1961-65.

Those who return from the mountain in Garabandal will have seen the glory of the Lord and be eager to sound His glory to all the world. The glory of Zion, the glory of the New Pentecost prayed for by Pope John XXIII as he opened the Second Vatican Council and again by Pope Paul VI when he drew it to a close, will flow over the whole Church and the entire world.

The third event promised by Our Lady is a Permanent Sign that will remain forever as a result of the Great Miracle. It will be of supernatural origin and something that has never been seen before on Earth. Conchita has written: *"A sign of the Miracle, which will be possible to film or televise, will remain forever at the pines."*

A permanent, visible supernatural sign will remain at the pines until the end of time. It has been likened to a column of smoke or a ray of sunlight but is not either one. As a result of the Miracle, Russia and other countries will be converted. The Permanent Sign that the Blessed Virgin promised will remain at Garabandal after the Miracle at the nine pines at the base of the surrounding mountains. Little has been revealed about the nature of this sign, but we know the following details: it will remain at the pines until the end of the world.

It will remind us forever of the Great Miracle, which will center on that very spot. Anyone who wishes, will be able to go to Garabandal after the Miracle and see the sign. It will recall to our minds that God summons the world to repentance and holiness. The Israelites were continually reminded by the fiery cloud called the Shekinah Glory hovering over the Meeting Tent that God was with them, leading them to holiness and to the Holy Land. The sign will be with us like that cloud of God's glory, reminding us that the Lord is leading us to holiness and Heaven and that He will not tolerate idolatry among His people. Because it will remain there until the end of time, it will also insist by its presence that the world will indeed one day end, and that Jesus will come again, *"but they will have to give an account to Him who is ready to judge the living and the dead"* (1 Peter 4:5).

Mystical Numbers — Our Lady is Planning on Saving the World

Numbers can also be a sign, a marker for an event. For the Hebrews of the Old Testament, numbers were important to understand God's will. As the New fulfills the Old, Our Lady also would use numbers as signs to mark an event. Numbers are often a signpost to the faithful, and meaningless to the uniformed. Might numbers also be prophetic for future dates? No one can deny the numbers 12 and 40 are important numbers in Scripture, and you would not be into a hysterical numerology thought process.

Fatima is just one example of that. Everything that was told to the Fatima children happened, and her appearances were on the 13th of the month. It was on the 13th of the month of Adar Queen Esther interceded to save her people from annihilation (Esther 9) and that number 13th is still an important date to send signal graces for those willing to listen.

Also of importance is the significance of the number 18. The 18th is a number that has meaning to the Jewish people. It signifies life, and many observant Jews tithe in increments of eighteen as they feel the number will bring blessings and good fortune if they acknowledge God in their giving. The 18th of the month is when several important messages were given at Garabandal. On October 18, 1961, Our Lady said, "already *the cup is filling*," and on June 18, 1965, she said, "*before the cup was filling up, now it is flowing over.*"

In a book written by Mirjana named *My Heart Will Triumph,* that was released August 15, 2016, Mirjana states that March **18** will be a date of great significance that we will only understand when the events prophesied at Medjugorje start to happen. She also mentions specifically August 2 as another important date. The Church celebrates August 2nd as the feast day of Our Lady of the Angels. The Blessed Mother used to appear to Mirjana on the 2nd of every month, when she regularly received messages she conveyed to the world, and annually on her birthday of March **18**[th]. However, during the Covid pandemic, the 2nd of the month appearances ceased.

Our Blessed Mother appeared **18** times to Bernadette Soubirous at Lourdes, France. These apparitions began February 11, 1858 when the Blessed Mother prayed the Rosary with Bernadette. On February **18**, the Blessed Mother spoke for the first time and said, *"I do not promise to make you happy in this life, but in the next."* It was at Lourdes where the Blessed Mother said: *"I am the Immaculate Conception."* The **18**[th] and final apparition occurred on July 16, 1858 on the Feast of Our Lady of Mount Carmel, a sacred site to the Jewish people as well as Christians.

Mirjana said, *"only when the things contained in the secrets start to happen will the world understand why she chose the **18**[th] of the month… When everything starts happening, then you will be able to understand why the **18**[th] of March, why every second of the month, and why Wednesdays and Fridays are days of fasting. The significance of the date will be clear."*

Are these dates connected throughout these apparitions? Again, only when these events happen, will we fully understand the importance of the numbers 2 and 13, and possibly the 18th, as having some sort of great significance. It could be presumptuous to say the dates of the 18th, and the 2nd are directly linked at Garabandal and Medjugorje, and also foolish to say they are not. The honest answer is, maybe they are. It is obvious there are many similarities since the number 2 and 18 have such a common thread in both apparitions.

The Likely Reaction From the Rabbis

For cultured Jews and Rabbis, a thorough knowledge of the Scriptures is a large measure of their religious life. In Israel, whatever their beliefs, all citizens have studied the Hebrew Scriptures as a text of Hebrew classical literature. Whether or not they consider it as divinely inspired and obey it, they still know it. Signs from Heaven are a staple for Heaven to communicate with people. If one were to just indiscriminately open the Bible, we would see in many stories how the Lord is using either signs and wonders or just signs as a marker for an event, something to look for to validate what He is saying for the people to understand. The Warning, the Miracle and the Permanent Sign, are such events where something is foretold and then it happens.

Jews know that it has been prophetically announced that, *"your sons and your daughters will prophesy."* (Song of Songs 3:6; Joel 2:28; and Acts 2:17-21). Thanks to the media that will cover the event, they will know at once that Catholic girls have announced in advance that in a Catholic village in Catholic Spain a Permanent Sign will remain *"para siempre"* — forever. They will be interested, especially the Sephardim, the Spanish Jews. Their interest will be extreme and lasting, because the Miracle will be a sign for them.

They know if the Permanent Sign is a pillar of smoke by day and a fire by night, this will be prophetic sign of enormous impact. During the apparitions a burning bush and a pillar of smoke has appeared. Many pilgrims who have visited Medjugorje and other shrines have seen a large white luminous cross appear on the mountain. These phenomena may be factors in the Miracle or Permanent Sign. It is interesting to note that at Medjugorje, there are ten secrets which allegedly deal with warnings, a miracle, a permanent sign, and preannounced events. Conchita will announce the day of the Miracle eight days in advance.

Consistent Themes

There are important links between LaSalette, France; Fatima, Portugal; Akita, Japan; and Medjugorje, Bosnia, and others to Garabandal. There are similar themes: the importance and power of the Rosary and of the priesthood; the emphasis on the Eucharist; the presence of angels the emphasis placed on the sacraments; the secrets given which will be revealed at later dates; the urgent calls for prayer and penance; the emergence of a main visionary among the children; and visions of coming calamities unless there is repentance. Garabandal is yet another instance where the Blessed Mother points to the absolute basic fundamental tenets of the faith.

The Miracle of Garabandal is different from any event at any other apparition site, yet similar in some respects. We do know a Permanent Sign of some sort will be left at valid apparition sites around the world, and whether it is the same sign would be speculation on anyone's part. To connect them as the same event may be valid and possibly not. Each apparition site has to stand on its own to be authentic after a thorough investigation by the Church.

Understanding the heart and mind of God, and what He is doing in our day enables one to absorb more freely without constraint what Heaven is doing now at this point in history. It appears we are seeing the confluence of world-wide phenomena culminating in events people are barely able to comprehend. But then again, God is a God of the supernatural, and the Lord said, *"My thoughts are not your thoughts, neither are your ways my ways"* (Isaiah 55:8). The major apparition sites that are Church approved, amplify one another and build on each other for a clearer understanding much in the same way knowledge of Scripture does for a person. In time, you get the mind of the Blessed Mother and understand her ways, and her appearances become like modern day epistles to edify and exhort the people of God. You see patterns in her appearances based on enormous amounts of information. As Saint Thomas Aquinas said in Summa Theologiae, *"Grace does not destroy nature, but fulfills its potential."*

We are literally on the threshold of events prophesied at Garabandal that have never been seen before in all history. Overflowing with signs where the New validates the Old, and vice versa, the events are so fantastic no one could deny they come from God when they happen. The events are very plausible if one bundles all the cogent facts together, and the events at Garabandal will be the only thing in the world that can turn mankind around from self-destruction.

The Chastisement

A Chastisement is contingent upon the world's response to the Warning and the Great Miracle which has been prophesied. During July of 1962, Conchita, Mari-Loli, and Jacinta were shown a vision of the impending chastisement. This is often referred to as *"The Night of Screams."* Our Lady told the visionaries that, if we do not heed her warnings and mankind does not change after the Warning and Miracle, God will send the Chastisement. In a note Conchita stated: *"The punishment is conditioned upon whether or not mankind heeds the messages of the Blessed Virgin Mary."* Conchita said in her diary: *"If the world changes, the Chastisement can be averted."* In describing the vision of the Chastisement, Mari-Loli said that she saw people throwing themselves into the sea, but instead of putting the fire out, it *"would be worse than having fire on top of us — fire underneath us and fire all around us. It seemed to make them burn more."* The blood curdling screams of the three seers during the **Night of Screams** prompted the entire village of Garabandal to go to Confession the following day.

Conclusion

What is it in an individual that makes him or her open to all of the Blessed Mother's phenomena? After decades of observation, I think it is that the people who gravitate to her messages are open to what God is willing to freely give, and they simply say — YES. Since Mary as a young girl from Nazareth gave her yes, her fiat to the angel Gabriel that she would be the Mother of God, then God was able to accomplish His will for the salvation and redemption of the world. By saying YES, the Lord can work in our life. When there is surrender, there is growth. Surrender brings openness, and thus growth. Your YES is surrender. As Jesus said, *"Unless a grain of wheat falls into the ground and dies, it remains alone; but if it dies, it bears fruit"* (John 12:24). Only when our ego submits to the will of Heaven, is there growth.

The prophesied events at Garabandal will change history like possibly no other event since the Incarnation of Jesus. Msgr. Eugenio Beitia Aldazabal (deceased 1985) who was bishop of San Tander, Spain from 1962-1965 when the apparitions took place, said after reading a letter that Conchita gave to him, and then told his secretary, *"if these girls are not insane, this event alone (most likely the Miracle) is comparable to the death of Christ."*

The story of Garabandal is unlike any other apparition in history. Although the Blessed Mother seldom speaks in Scripture, her words, *"Do whatever He tells you"* (John 2:5) at the wedding feast of Cana are most significant. She is always pointing to her Son and that is her most common theme of authentic apparition sites globally.

No one can doubt that the confluence of events in the world has pushed us beyond the tipping point. The world is out of control, and many people are anxious and discouraged, bordering on despair. Uncertainty, stress, and anxiety grip households. However, as Mirjana says in her book, *"Our Lady is preparing us for everything that is going to take place in the world. She is training us for victory. When the events in the secrets begin, everything will be clear."* Heaven has a plan and needs our cooperation to fulfill that plan. Garabandal is a big part of that plan, and those following the messages world-wide know it. God spoke to His people in the past, and He does so today. *"God is the same yesterday, today, and forever"* (Hebrews 13:8).

As predicted, there has been confusion and controversy in regard to the spread of the message of Garabandal. Jesus told Conchita on February 13, 1966: *"Don't worry yourself with whether people believe or do not believe.... I shall do everything. But I will also give you suffering. I will be with whoever suffers for me.... You will have much to suffer for few people will believe you."* Both the suffering of Conchita and the other visionaries, and the lack of belief in the apparitions were foretold by Our Lady. The Lord said, *"they hated me before thy hated you"* (John 15:18). We are now in a period of waiting and expectation in regard to the prophesied events of Garabandal. During this time let us all in faith, while living and spreading the messages, pray and make sacrifices and place all in the hands of Our Lord. Keep up your courage and remember there is nothing that so enlarges the capacity of the heart for God as does suffering and putting our trust in Him. He is the King of Love, Mercy, and Peace. One who finds God, finds peace.

JESUS I TRUST IN YOU

Other Works by Ted Flynn

The Great Reset, The Globalist Plan vs. Heaven's Victory, 2022, 280 pages. Heaven has their own version of a global reset that will change the world on their terms like people could never imagine. Heaven defines their target that they will dismantle to turn the tide of evil we see around us. Heaven through Scripture has given us a prescription for interior peace, and where our refuge lies. Very practical.

Diabolical Disorientation, The Roots of the Crisis in the Church, the Family, the Nation, and the Culture, 2020.

Essays on the direction of the church, and the family in turbulent times with a unique orthodox Marian theme and how to thrive in times of crisis.

The Great Transformation, Finding Peace of Soul in Troubled Times, 2015. A description of how the world was being transformed before our very eyes based on many data points.

The Thunder of Justice, The Warning, The Miracle, The Chastisement, And The Era of Peace, 2010, revised and updated from the original 1993/2010 best seller. Translated in 6 languages. Ted & Maureen Flynn. An overview of the major and most impactful Marian apparition sites in history and their primary messages. Heavy emphasis on Garabandal and the Warning and the Great Miracle.

Idols in the House, 2002. Shows the destiny of a family, and thus the nation that abandons the first commandment of honoring God first. Examples from Scripture and prior civilizations. Proven to be prophetic to America and the world today.

The Hope of the Wicked, The Master Plan to Rule the World, 2000. The political philosophy and ideology of rulers in the world in their own words (over 1,200 footnotes), and how they want to govern the world. We are now living what they proposed generations ago. Provides a description of the Deep State before the term was ever used. A book 20 years ahead of its time.

Key to the Triumph, The Final Marian Dogma of Co-redemptrix, Mediatrix, Advocate, 1997, DVD. Filmed in Italy with the words of leading individuals and clergy on the importance of the Dogma being proclaimed.

Prophecy and the New Times, 1995, DVD. Providing information from leading authorities and mystics from the apparitions in the Thunder of Justice, it is as informative as when it was first made.

The Global Warning, an Illumination of the Conscience of Mankind, by Maureen Flynn, 2011. Details the Warning and the Great Miracle and what it will mean for mankind.

See **Sign.org** (Signs and Wonders for Our Time) for a greater selection of books and other spiritual products. (703) 707-0799

About the Author

Ted Flynn is an author and Executive Producer of several films. He is the founder and president of MaxKol Communications, Inc. (1994). He attended the University of Massachusetts/Amherst, American University, the University of Fribourg, Switzerland, and the London School of Economics (England).

He was Chief Economist of a government agency. He has worked in consulting, been active in not for profits, real estate development, and energy development. He is President and founder of a publishing company. He worked in Poland on retrofitting power plants after the fall of the Berlin Wall, and then Belarus after the fall of USSR during glasnost, distributing food aid with funds from USAID and the Department of Agriculture. He has spoken in over 700 venues in the world on the types of subjects addressed in this book and previous works, and has given over 300 radio and television interviews. He has traveled to over 50 countries in his career. He can be reached at: **tflynn333@icloud.com**.